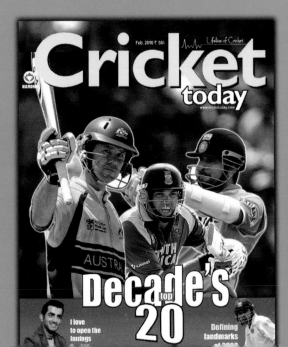

WORLD BEATERS

WORLD CUP 2011

PRESENTED BY

DIAMOND BOOKS

© Publisher

Published 2011

DIAMOND POCKET BOOKS PVT. LTD.
X-30, Okhla Industrial Area
Phase-2, New Delhi-110020
Phone-011-41611861 Fax-011-41611866
E-mail: sales@diamondpublication.com
www.dpb.in

Cover & Book Design by
Santosh Kushwaha

Picture courtesy:
AP, Pradeep Mandhani

Printed in India by
Best Photo Offset
New Delhi, India

Foreword

I was all of six when I first saw images of a jubilant Kapil Dev lifting the World Cup Trophy amidst loud cheers and passionate exclaims. While I was still too young to fathom the enormity of the occasion, it undoubtedly left an indomitable mark on my mind and spurred a spiral of events that changed life completely. Perhaps, it's on that day of June 1983 that the thought of playing Cricket and the dream of lifting that coveted Trophy first germinated. It would be fair to say that if Kapil Dev hadn't done the unthinkable 28 years ago, I wouldn't have picked up the bat, at all.

I grew up, played for India, but my dream of India claiming the title once again, kept eluding me every four years. In fact, Australia's hegemony over World Cricket ensured that I even stopped fancying the dream of regaining the title, for over a decade the competition was never about winning the title but being the second best. Would I ever see India at the top of the World again? Well, I wasn't sure. Yes, we had become one of the most formidable teams in the world but our records in the ICC events weren't awe-inspiring to say the least.

But 2011 started on a different pitch. We had started winning matches against every opposition and under all conditions. To add to that, the World Cup tournament was slated to happen in our backyard, our turf, our fortress. We had the best possible batting line-up at our disposal. Our bowling looked slightly weaker but had mostly delivered and above all, Australian cricket was on an obvious decline. While we had both the resources and the resolve, winning the World Cup was about winning crucial moments as much as not losing decisive phases. Did we have it in us to not fumble even once? We knew that even the slightest of complacency or a trivial goof-up could make us miss the bus. At the outset, I had given India a fair chance of winning this edition, but I'd be lying if I said that I didn't know it was coming, and for real.

We started strongly against Bangladesh but before we could savour the moment, we slipped against England. We stood up again only to bite the dust against the Proteas. A few chinks in our armoury got exposed in the process. Our fielding wasn't top class; our bowling was relying too much on Zaheer and our batting flopped more than once towards the death overs. Would it be the proverbial slip between the cup and the lip, I wondered!

But little did we know that these were just the right challenges which primed us well for the knock-outs. Yuvraj started blossoming with the ball to rescue Dhoni in the bowling department, Sachin's hunger and enthusiasm rubbed off to the entire team, Zaheer didn't disappoint even once when assigned the job to break a partnership and believe it or not, our fielding rose to another level.

The tough battle of technical supremacy against Australia was won with a lot of flair. The tougher battle of holding the nerves against arch-rivals Pakistan was won with a lot of grit and determination. And the toughest battle of them all, one about dominance and honour against Sri Lanka was won with a statement – We're the best team in the World, We are the champions!

Aakash Chopra
Cricketer

Acknowledgment

At the outset I thank Sreelata S Yellamrazu and Vimal Kumar (IBN7) for their unstinted and selfless support in the writing of this book. They have helped me with information and articles, not to forget the time they have devoted on improving the content. They are the co-authors of this book.

I take this opportunity to thank Mr Manish Verma, Editor-in-chief of *Diamond Magazines* for granting me permission to go ahead with this project. I am indebted to *Diamond Magazines* for providing me the opportunity to travel and cover India's entire World cup matches at different venues. I take immense pride in being part of such a great organization.

I thank Aakash Chopra for penning the Foreword. I have known him since more than a decade and over these years our relationship has grown with time. He is a genius and the most technically sound batsman I have ever seen along with Rahul Dravid.

I cannot forget the cooperation extended by my fellow colleagues Mohd Asim, Ajay Raj and Lalita Adhikari. This book would have been incomplete without their support.

I am indebted to Pervez Qaiser, the statistician from Delhi. He has established himself as one of the finest and reliable statisticians in the field of cricket. As a member of the Association of Cricket Statisticians, he was best qualified to provide us the Records and Milestones achieved by the Indian players during the World Cup.

Without the support of Associated Press and Pradeep Mandhani, the section on photographs would have lacked quality. Pradeep Mandhani, the no. 1 sports photographer of our country, has been in the field of cricket since more than three decades and is respected a lot by the players. It was nice of him to provide us a few pictures.

Finally, I cannot forget to mention my lovely wife, Mamta Pandey. A true guide, she has been the greatest source of strength for me right through my good and bad days.

Rakesh Pandey
Editor – Cricket Today

CONTENTS

Entire India

Celebrates

Clockwise: Fans take to the streets in Mumbai after India won the World Cup.
The wait of 28 long years is over for Indian fans.
There were joyous scenes in New Delhi as revellers celebrated throughout the night.

From top: Kolkata celebrates India's World Cup triumph.
The Bachchan's also joined the party in the streets of Mumbai.

Clockwise: Traffic jam at midnight was a common affair throughout India after the historical victory. Celebrations of fans spread right upto Jammu.
Fans bursting crackers & dancing to the tune of drums in Gwalior.

Clockwise: The European style victory celebration happened for the first time in India, with fans shouting slogans sitting on top of their vehicles.

It was Diwali time in Allahabad after India answered the battle cry of one billion people.

Indian flags are waved on a street in Guwahati.

Clockwise: Holding flags & dancing, the people of Mangalore added their bit to the celebrations.
The night sky were illuminated with fire crackers.
Chandigarh celebrates India's victory over Pakistan in the semi-final.
It's 3 in the night but party is still on in Mumbai.

For a billion strong fan following, the Indian cricket team is a matter of envy for nations unable to fathom the cricket fervor in its fanatical people. Facing an opposition like India in the backdrop of such crowd can be an overwhelming experience indeed. But for the ardent Indian fans, their passions found no boundaries as Indian cricket breached history for a second time in twenty-eight years. The lifting of the ICC Cricket World Cup 2011 was not only a momentous occasion for the Indian cricket team but also, for the entire nation who put

A Cup Won by Every Indian

their personal agendas on hold with the sole aim to cheer their team to the trophy.

The moment Mahendra Singh Dhoni hit the final six of the tournament to make a memorable end to India's successful journey in the ICC Cricket World Cup 2011, the nation was left in shock and then in jubilation, the likes of which quite unprecedented in its style and magnitude. The euphoria of the entire nation managed to surpass the fervent prayers that trailed India from their first match against Bangladesh to every city across the nation as the team traversed the road to ultimately being crowned the champions of the ICC Cricket World Cup 2011.

The celebrations thereafter continued on for the next forty-eight hours in a frenzy where time held little relevance. Fireworks rendered the air, giving one the feeling of dawn even before the sun

Fans in Delhi gathered on the streets after India won the World Cup.

could rise. And while some would say that Diwali had arrived early, it still would not fully express the manner in which the nation expressed its joy, gratitude and adulation for the Indian cricket team.

And the party simply refused to die down, forcing the police and security personnel to relax the rules, following the match until the sun came up. If members of the Indian cricket team found it hard to sleep the night prior to the match, the people of the nation found sleep elusive as they took the revelry to the roads, sharing the joy with strangers and mingling with

people of prominence who shed their security and privacy so as not to miss out on the emotions that seemed to flow rather freely on the streets.

This party did not need a venue. And it did not need a theme to set the mood. The party has been in planning ever since the ICC Cricket World Cup 2011 got underway. Prayers were said, religion did not matter. People planned their attire even if there was no stadium to go to. And work was planned and schedules re-laid to make sure nothing came in the way in their stellar attempts to get behind every ball in the

match that India played.

Indian fans have been carrying their candle of hope for the aspirations of the Indian cricket team reliving the memories of the first time India won the World Cup format in 1983 under the captaincy of Kapil Dev. The dream to realize it once more has been cherished in edition after edition with fervor that has sometimes seen the extreme of emotions when people invest all of their emotions behind the team only to be bitterly disappointed and devastated when India failed to cross the final hurdle. That though has not stopped them from dreaming or praying.

Amongst the many ways that fans took the tension of team India's hurdles was offering of prayers in temples, mosques and churches across the country before and after. As India moved further, the prayers only became more intense, the havans and the deities invoked with greater diligence than at perhaps most other times in one's life. For a country with a religious bent of mind, it would seem only natural that cricketers are revered like deities when they succeed but also, that they are prayed for in the most sincerest of fan adulation seen anywhere in the world. In the final stretch the religious fanaticism took on cricket overtones, and not just amongst the Indian cricketers.

"Sick leaves leave health officials worried!" That should have been the headline given that the number of absentees in the office had risen significantly as India progressed into the end stages of the tournament. If one had to truly understand how heavily the people of India were invested in the team, one had to look no further than watch how the nations operated on the days when India was playing in the tournament. Particularly as the tournament moved from the league phase into the knock outs, the frenzy took on a mo-

From top: Enthusiastic cricket fans perform a special puja praying for their team's victory.
A hairdresser paints the hair of a fan, styled to resemble the World Cup trophy.
A fan has the Indian tri color painted on his face.

tion of its own. One can safely vouch that many of the offices witnessed either a low turnout or distracted agendas as employers thought it wise to set up a television set within the premises than have people stay home and apply leave of absence. For those that did turn up, business of socializing was at an all time low because the clients would not indulge either.

Bustling streets wore deserted looks, and the shopping centres, malls and flea markets bore no sign of the kind of attention they enjoy like bees to honey. Movie theatres found no takers, even as the actors themselves took time off work to follow the team to the stadiums, while hotels and community centres decided to enhance business, camaraderie and bonhomie by screening India's matches on giant screens. People gathered to experience stadium-like viewing experiences.

Those that were forced to keep the shop shutters open opted for television sets to ensure that they or their employees did not miss out on the action. Shop owners gave first account details of just how quiet their business had been on the day. Their reason for not shutting down? To cater to clients with urgent necessities that could not be avoided despite the match. Banks chose to give their employees half day leave while certain offices operated in the early hours to allow the employees to return home in time for the match. There were even reports of patients who decided to postpone their surgery and support the team instead.

By the time India reached the final, the frenzy took on serious proportions to the extent that the Government of India chose to declare Saturday, the day of the final, a government holiday for their employees, prompting several offices to take the cue and let their staff off for the day. The only ones perhaps stuck in the ill timing of events were board students who were

**From top: Celebs at the World Cup final.
Actor Aamir Khan & wife Kiran Rao share company with business tycoon Mukesh Ambani & wife Nita Ambani.
Actors Abhishek Bachchan & Bipasha Basu during the match against South Africa in Nagpur.**

On the invitation of the Indian Prime Minister, Manmohan Singh, the Pakistan Prime Minister, Yousaf Raza Gilani, shared the hospitality box in Mohali as India and Pakistan went head on in the match.

forced to attend their examinations that could not be rescheduled. For a cricket fanatic country, perhaps that was the only let down in the scenario that the World Cup schedule happened to coincide with the students of high schools, colleges and universities because it robbed them off the full experience of letting these images of India's success be fully imprinted on their minds.

However, the timing of the quarter-finals, semi final and final posed no problems for actors and members of the film industry, politicians as well as industrialists who turned up in hospitality boxes across stadiums, thronging like the crowds that usually throng them for attention, and revealing the side to them that made them no different from the common man sharing the same stadium space, albeit on a different leave of ambience and amenities.

As India inched closer to the finals, politicians of the highest level shared stadium space as the public en masse. On the invitation of the Indian Prime Minister, Manmohan Singh, the Pakistan Prime Minister, Yousaf Raza Gilani, shared the hospitality box in Mohali as India and Pakistan went head on in

the match that would determine the second finalist to join Sri Lanka in the ICC Cricket World Cup 2011 final at the Wankhede Stadium in Mumbai. The problems with the Kochi franchisee did not stop Shashi Tharoor and his new wife, Sunanda Pushkar, making their presence felt like prominent leaders of political parties who left behind their political differences across borders in the common cause of supporting team India.

But the India Pakistan match did not draw ministers and members of Parliament alone. The match saw not only an unprecedented demand of match tickets but also, Bollywood actors such as Aamir Khan who cancelled plans of hosting their World Cup party at home because they could not resist the opportunity to watch the action live in Mohali. Preity Zinta (Bollywood actress and co owner of the Kings XI Punjab in the IPL) was a knock out herself in the hospitality box, dressing in traditional Indian wear and sporting bangles whose colours represented the Indian flag tricolor, a fashion trend that was replicated by dozens across the country through saris, accessories, et al amongst the fairer sex.

As India progressed further into the

knockout stages, they attracted the common man as they did prominent industrialists in the likes of Mukesh Ambani and his wife Nita Ambani, Vijay Mallya amongst several others who made it their business to attend the match in full attendance of friends and family, leading to a frenzy of flying plans.

Those not as privileged to witness the match in the stadium, and that includes a sizeable number of the common man, made their own arrangements to ensure that India's campaign in the World Cup was not something they would miss to rue later. What really puts matters in perspective is that amongst the many people who chose to forgo their day's work included a sizeable number of daily wage workers, for whom not working for a day makes living and supporting families a strenuous affair. But that could not come in the way of their prayer and support for the team. It led taxi and auto rickshaws unions to announce in advance that travel services would be hit, and it were true as roads were barren without traffic, vehicles and pollution.

There was no sign of life on the streets while the match was on. But the enduring image of Dhoni hitting the winning runs will be intermingled of the sudden thronging of

Clockwise: Congress President Sonia Gandhi & son Rahul watching India's semi-final clash against Pakistan at Mohali. Before the all important Indo-Pak clash at Mohali. Sachin's greatest fan, Sudhir Gautam, waves the national flag.

the streets by people that cut across all barriers of class, caste, religion, race and creed. How else can one explain how Sonia Gandhi, leader of the ruling government party, should find herself at India Gate, stepping out of the vehicle and matching steps with the revelers well into the night? How does one explain the number of Bollywood actors joining one another in and outside the stadium, mingling amongst cricket fans and the parties that continued well into the wee hours of the morning if only to feel free and be able to share those emotions with the public?

To an outsider unfamiliar with the sport and trend of fans in India, it may seem not only bordering on madness but also, endearing in the love of the people and their expression of it. It is perhaps why some of the foreign members of the press and the electronic media have made it their business to cover more than the proceedings of the after match or a discussion of the match itself.

The fans may not pocket the millions but that has never been the motivation for cricket fans. With national pride is at stake, it painted a terrific picture of sport being a unifying force. This victory for team India is priceless in every sense of the word. It can strengthen the confidence of the players and at the same time, it can weaken them in their

The fans may not pocket the millions but that has never been the motivation for cricket fans.

knees with humility of such tremendous fan backing. Captains often say, it is only a game, you win some, you lose some. On the 2nd of April (or on any day when India strode out on to the cricket pitch during the tournament), the game meant more than a contest between ball and ball and more than at any time when national interests dominated the sport. It tug at the heartstrings of a billion people, and every image relived brings a little song and dance amongst the people who are unable to get over the euphoria that has taken over the nation.

Just when cricket though it could not outdo itself in the country, it breached new ground. If this is what a rare World Cup victory means to the people, imagine what it would mean for team India to

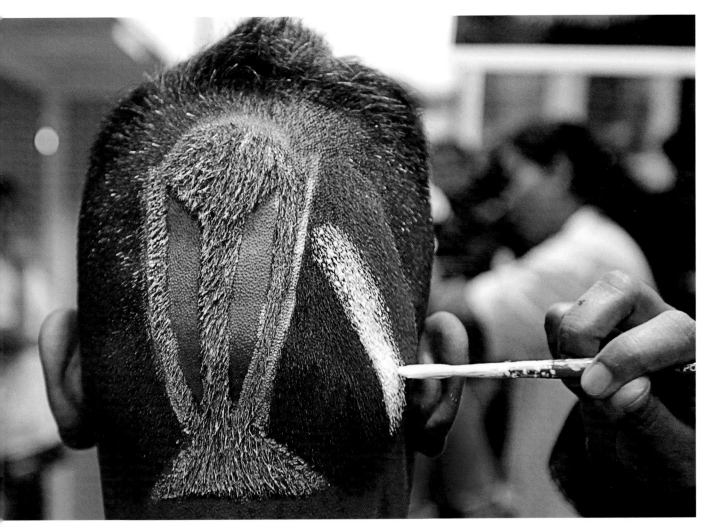

From top: Yet another World Cup trophy shape haircut by a fan.
A fan with her face painted 'chak de' & looking to spur team India in their quest for the title.
Actor Shahid Kapoor cheering for India at the finals in Mumbai.

be starting a whole new chapter in cricket's glorious history! And what would history be if not for the people? The people who rallied behind their team despite their own personal odds need to be saluted as do the players who did the nation so proud. This was a rare moment in history when people of the nation gathered as one, opened their hearts and let their emotions take care on the realization of a goal, a long cherished dream that will now share the stage of an incident that inspired some of the cricketers themselves twenty-eight years ago! 😊

India's Road to
World Cup Glory

Journey

Vs Bangladesh

Vs England

Vs Ireland

Vs Netherlands

Vs South Africa

Vs West Indies

Vs Australia

Vs Pakistan

Vs Sri Lanka

" With only one loss and a tie in the entire tournament, India's progression in the tournament was not without blemish. "

In the triumph and jubilation of India's ultimate success at the ICC Cricket World Cup 2011, the thrill of a rewind to retrace India's footsteps in the tournament speaks volumes of how team has evolved in the tournament, coming into their own, fortifying their self belief in moments otherwise of self doubt, and keeping their nerve and the edge in the toughest battles against their neighbours to emerge as champions.

With only one loss and a tie in the entire tournament, India's progression in the tournament was not without blemish. But it was certainly the development of an interesting chain of patterns as India showed their vulnerable side in patches in the course of the group stage but also, the wherewithal to overcome them in victory which is a hallmark of champion sides. What is remarkable is that as the tournament progressed, particularly in the knock phase, India kept getting stronger and more determined, counting on talent but sailing through and passing out with flying colours in the end with mental fortitude, presence of mind, captain's intuition and insight and strong backroom staff presence (some may also add, a certain member who goes by the name Yuvraj Singh).

Without much ado, here are some of the most remarkable moments of India's journeys in the ICC Cricket World Cup 2011, reaching a crescendo with India winning the final to emulate Kapil Dev's Indian squad's 1983 World Cup success.

GROUP STAGE

Vs Bangladesh

Sehwag and Kohli sink Bangladesh in opener

V irender Sehwag put his best foot forward but the same could not be said about India's bowling. India's concerns going into the tournament gave them a rusty appearance as Bangladesh made a case for themselves. Sreesanth was easily the most expensive bowler of the day, conceding fifty-three runs off just five overs while Munaf Patel brought forth the surprise element package by emerging as the leading wicket taker with four wickets.

Sehwag began in typical, hard-hitting fashion, getting India off to a flier.

Sreesanth was easily the most expensive bowler of the day.

That Bangladesh ended up making 283 chasing India's colossal total of 370 at the Shere Bangla National Stadium in Mirpur must now seem like ages ago. A forty-five day tournament can do that. However, what is indelible is the fact that Sehwag scored 175 runs off only 140 balls, threatened to knock down Sachin Tendulkar's top ODI score of 200 runs, and sent shudders down the spines of those who had underestimated India's prowess, particularly with the bat, coming into the tournament. Virat Kohli represented the next generation of Indian cricketers and suitably made his case on this platform with a century in a 203 run partnership with Sehwag for the third wicket that batted the hosts out of the match.

But Bangladesh's batting was praiseworthy in the context of things, with the first wicket yielding fifty-three runs in the first seven overs. Tamim Iqbal showed the way with seventy runs while the Bangladesh captain, Shakib Al Hasan, scored a half century to show Bangladesh was a decent batting side, with the top six batsmen all getting starts. India's bowling appeared to be missing Praveen Kumar and his replacement fared hardly better to suffer the ignominy of warming the bench right until the final. India though had the cushion of runs to overshadow Bangladesh making a decent reputation for themselves in World Cup matches, although unable to replicate the result against India from four years ago.

Vs England

Epic encounter ends in thrilling tie

Four brilliant top order partnerships and India failed to get their finish in order. 134 runs between Sachin Tendulkar and Gautam Gambhir had England eating out of India's hands at the M. Chinnaswamy Stadium in Bengaluru. Tendulkar edged closer to his hundred international centuries with a belligerent century to boot while Gambhir and Yuvraj Singh followed up with half centuries of their own.

However, the game changer was on as Tim Bresnan made up with his five-for to compensate for an uncharacteristic tournament from James Anderson, who went for almost ten runs an over in the match. Bresnan burst India's bubble when he took Yuvraj Singh and Mahendra Singh Dhoni out of the equation off successive overs with India's score on 305. With no one to finish the game deserving of the death overs, India settled for 338.

Team India thought they had enough runs on board until they saw the England captain, Andrew Strauss, in fluent motion and picking runs at will. On a benign pitch, India's bowlers struggled to find their feet and Piyush Chawla was losing the battle to make a case for his surprise selection at the World Cup. England had this match virtually sealed at 281 with the captain going great guns on 150 and Ian Bell providing healthy support with sixty-nine runs in a match-complexion-changing partnership of 170 runs for the third wicket.

But then the match turned on its head once more when Zaheer Khan was brought

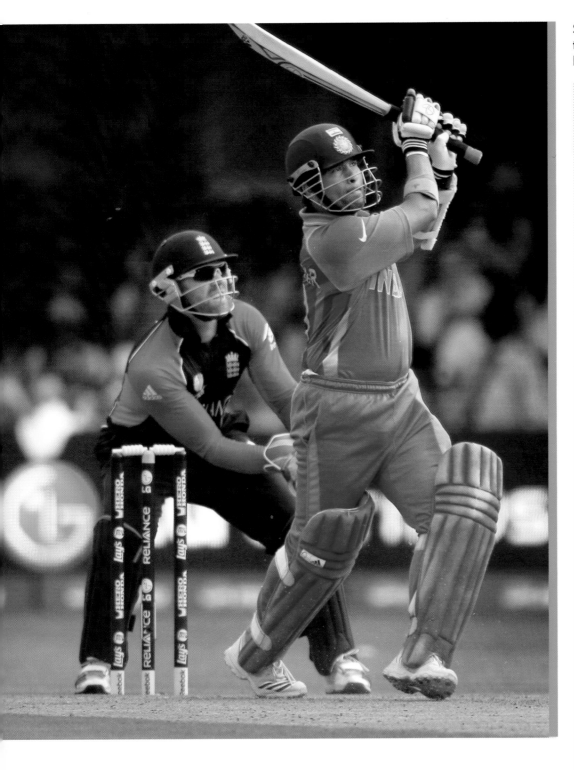

Sachin sends the ball into the stands during his 103-ball century.

The match turned on its head once more when Zaheer Khan was brought back into the attack.

back into the attack. The Indian spearhead shocked England when he dismissed Strauss and Bell in the forty-third over and returned the next over to take the experienced Paul Collingwood out to add to England's drama. It was still a 50:50 equation as the match went down to the wire with India's alertness following Zak's triple strike brought the match to a thrilling tie, a result that hurt both teams who gave away the match from great batting positions.

Vs Ireland

All-round Yuvraj thrash hapless Ireland

Yuvraj fooled Ireland into reading his slower balls.

India faced a tough challenge from Ireland who refused to believe they were not one of the Test playing nations. Ireland once more zexposed India's weakness in the bowling attack with the spinners unable to take wickets to pull things back. 113 runs for the third wickets between the Ireland captain, William Porterfield, and Niall O'Brien stretched India in the field in the group match in Bengaluru. Porterfield was surprisingly calm as Ireland played a relatively sensible innings until the half way mark.

Ireland, however, came up against the innocuously looking part time bowler, Yuvraj Singh. Where the likes of Harbhajan Singh and Piyush Chawla were too silent, Yuvraj Singh sent Ireland on a jittery tale they managed to get to 122 runs with the loss of the two wickets early on. Yuvraj fooled Ireland into reading his slower balls, and the results began to tell in that Yuvraj picked up his first five-for to restrict Ireland to 207.

But Yuvraj's job was far from over. India struggled to make an impact on the proceedings, failing weak in the knees at two down for twenty-four and then again at four down for 100 when Mahendra Singh Dhoni and Yuvraj Singh combined forces with Virat Kohli's promising innings of thirty-four brought to end by an ill timed run out.

Yuvi celebrates his five-wicket haul with Raina & Kohli.

Ireland once more exposed India's weakness in the bowling attack.

The sixty-seven run partnership between the captain and Yuvraj who capped off his wicket taking ability on the day with a half century, however, was enough to ease tensions. It was left up to Yusuf Pathan to clear the ropes twice before India could rest easy after done away with a troublesome associate team, developing a reputation for tripping over established Test teams.

Vs Netherlands

Another Yuvi special rocks Netherlands

It was not entirely smooth sailing for India despite the fact that they were playing against the Netherlands. Their bowling was not up to the mark, but it was their batting that rocked the boat for a while Pieter Seelar left his mark on the match. Three wickets for Seelar changed the complexion of the chase after Sachin Tendulkar and Virender Sehwag revealed their aggressive streak to take to sixty-nine for no loss chasing Netherlands' 189 at the Ferozeshah Kotla in New Delhi.

Had Netherlands not lost their way to lose five wickets for only twenty-eight runs, India could have had a stiffer chase on their cards with Eric Szwarczynski and Wesley Barresi making a promise of a half century at the start. Yuvraj Singh got stuck into the proceedings as did Zaheer Khan for his three wickets and after looking strong on ninety-nine for two, Netherlands dragged their feet to 189, which could have been a lot worse had Peter Borren not scored those enterprising thirty-eight runs in a final ditch effort. It meant that Yuvraj Singh and Mahendra Singh Dhoni had to keep a close watch to finish the match with a sixty-one run partnership. A half century for Yuvraj Singh established who Dhoni's right hand man in the tournament was.

A half century for Yuvraj Singh established who Dhoni's right hand man in the tournament was.

Yuvi pulls one away during his third consecutive half-century.

Vs South Africa
Proteas prevail in the battle of nerves

Images of the Gwalior match where Sachin Tendulkar made the historic highest ODI score of 200 must have come flooding back as South Africa were in for a brutal assault on the senses by the opening pair of Virender Sehwag and Tendulkar. Graeme Smith, the South Africa, exhausted his bowling resources but to little avail. For 17.4 overs, South Africa thought they had lost plot and match for all practical purposes.

142 runs partnership, 115 runs for the second wicket and ironically the next best partnership in India's innings was 15 runs! That would explain precisely where India lost the opportunity to ram home a point. Instead the follow up Sehwag's seventy-three, Gautam Gambhir's sixty-nine and Tendulkar's stable, if not impressive, innings of 111 was disappointing poor on India's part who lost nine wickets for only twenty-nine runs.

Nagpur witnessed a pulsating run chase as South Africa, unlike India, put up a solid top order performance that percolated into the middle order. Half centuries from Hashim Amla, Jacques Kallis and AB de Villiers added weight to the 297 run chase while cameos were bleeding right through South Africa's middle-lower order with inconsistent bowling spells intermediating between stingy overs and overs where South Africa were able to capitalize on to narrow down the run chase, lusty hitting in the end from JP Duminy, Johan Botha and Robin Peterson pulling them through in a nerve racking match that spared only two balls.

Sachin & Sehwag gave a flying start to India.

India lost nine wickets for only twenty-nine runs.

Vs West Indies

Super Yuvraj floors Windies

India needed to win this match, not from the perspective of qualifying for the knock out round, already established through a complexity of results involving other teams, but to reestablish themselves as tournament favourites. A strong performance was the need of the hour. But even India would have been surprised by how easily they were able to land it in Chennai in what was hoped to be a pulsating affair at the M.A. Chidambaram Stadium.

India lost seven wickets for fifty runs in the end after Yuvraj Singh sent out a strong message with his century knock of 113 in a fighting partnership of 122 runs with Virat Kohli, after India lost Tendulkar and Gambhir early, Ravi Rampaul having a field day with five wickets.

To have lost the initiative for a third time in the tournament was leading to furious scribbling from scribes. It did not help as Devon Smith raised his hand and was doing a good appraisal of the situation with eighty-one run contribution off his own as West Indies appeared to be making light of India's efforts at 154 for two.

But if India had a mismanaged strategy towards the end of their innings, failing to capitalize on their death overs, West Indies sent the Caribbean into mourning once Zaheer Khan took charge of matters. Harbhajan Singh did a good holding job, an unsung role when he was not amongst the wickets tally, while Zaheer and Yuvraj Singh began to mop up the West Indies wickets. There was no strategy to the West Indies game plan and they went into complete meltdown once the anchor and architect in Devon Smith was out of the picture. Eight wickets for thirty-four runs was all it took to self destruct, this after they thought they had the match and the quarterfinals firmly within their sight at the half way mark. Eighty runs were enough to hide India's transgressions earlier in the day.

Yuvraj Singh sent out a strong message with his century knock of 113 in a fighting partnership of 122 runs with Virat Kohli.

Yuvi swings one into the leg side.

QUARTER FINAL

Yuvraj is ecstatic after hitting the winning runs.

Cameron White offered Zaheer Khan a return catch on 12.

Two half century partnerships between Sachin Tendulkar and Gautam Gambhir and between Gambhir and Virat Kohli kept India in the reckoning.

Vs Australia

Yuvi sends Aussies Packing

Australia were the three time defending champions going into the tournament although their mixed record overall in international cricket this season put them behind India amongst the favourites to win the trophy. In that context, victory for India would not only establish the notion of a new world order but also, importantly from the tournament point of view for team India, would take them within two steps of replicating the 1983 success.

Australia had several personal points to prove, including the captain himself. Ricky Ponting, however, was the Rock of Gibraltar on the day, coming through for his team at a critical juncture in the match where Australia lost Shane Watson early. Ponting's century in the time of crisis and his seventy run partnership with Brad Haddin for the third wicket was the anchor for Australia's campaign, with Yuvraj Singh putting vital brakes through the wickets of Haddin and Michael Clarke. Ravichandran Ashwin vindicated his selection with a couple of wickets but this would be his only match in the tournament.

Ravichandran Ashwin vindicated his selection with a couple of wickets.

Chasing Australia's 260 at the Sardar Patel Stadium in Motera, Ahmedabad, two half century partnerships between Sachin Tendulkar and Gautam Gambhir and between Gambhir and Virat Kohli kept India in the reckoning. Half centuries from Tendulkar and Gambhir laid the setting perfectly. But India still needed a solid innings to pull through. It came in the shape of the match winning seventy-four run sixth wicket partnership between Yuvraj Singh and Suresh Raina, playing his second World Cup match, after Dhoni fell cheaply. Yuvraj Singh's dogged determination in his fifty-seven runs and Raina's level headed thirty-four runs made sure that India's efforts at the top had not been in vain. The reigning champions had been vanquished. ✍

SEMI FINAL

Vs Pakistan

Sachin end Pakistan's magical run

This was the match that threatened to overshadow the finals that would follow it. An India versus Pakistan contest was not only mouthwatering but also, absorbing because it encompassed elements beyond the cricket boundary.

The high tensions in the match began to unravel as Sachin Tendulkar's good fortunes smiled upon him even as Pakistan faltered in the field. Dropping someone of the stature of Tendulkar is a cardinal sin and Pakistan were guilty of it on at least a couple of occasions. Pakistan paid the price for it as Tendulkar toughed it out for an innings of eighty-five, that almost brought him his 100th international century but more importantly lent the weight to the Indian batting scorecard.

Umar Gul and Pakistan missed the experience of Shoaib Akhtar. But Wahab Riaz blended nicely into the scheme of things to pick up five wickets to rattle India's middle order. Brief belligerence from Virender Sehwag at the top and a decent finish from Suresh Raina at the end gave India 260 runs to defend in an emotionally charged atmosphere in Mohali, Chandigarh.

India knew that stopping Pakistan from marching into the final would take outstanding fielding effort and impeccable bowling because they had underscored by at least twenty runs. Mahendra Singh Dhoni admitted later that he had misread the pitch because he went in for the traditional strategy of Mohali of three pace men when the pitch accorded favour for spin. But Pakistan continued to be benevolent, their suspect fragile batting order once again coming to the crease, despite beginning well with Mohammad Hafeez and Kamran Akmal. But if India had doubts, they were just as quickly put out of the mind as Pakistan's batsmen were forced into making some injudiciously

Yuvi, Sachin & Dhoni
celebrate as India
enter the finals.

Sachin Tendulkar's good fortunes smiled upon him even as Pakistan faltered in the field.

A decent finish from Suresh Raina at the end gave India 260 runs to defend.

Abdul Razzaq perished, missing a canny cutter from Munaf Patel.

Pakistan continued to remain second best to India in five one-on-one World Cup contests.

shot selections with the Indian bowlers sticking to their guns and the pressure of the situation. Gifted wickets by well set batsmen made it harder on the likes of Misbah ul Haq, who despite a half century, was forced to come to terms with another loss to India in a knock out contest. The Indian bowlers shared the spoils, with Yuvraj Singh turning his arms with increasingly regularity and contributing with the wickets as well. Pakistan continued to remain second best to India in five one-on-one World Cup contests.

FINAL

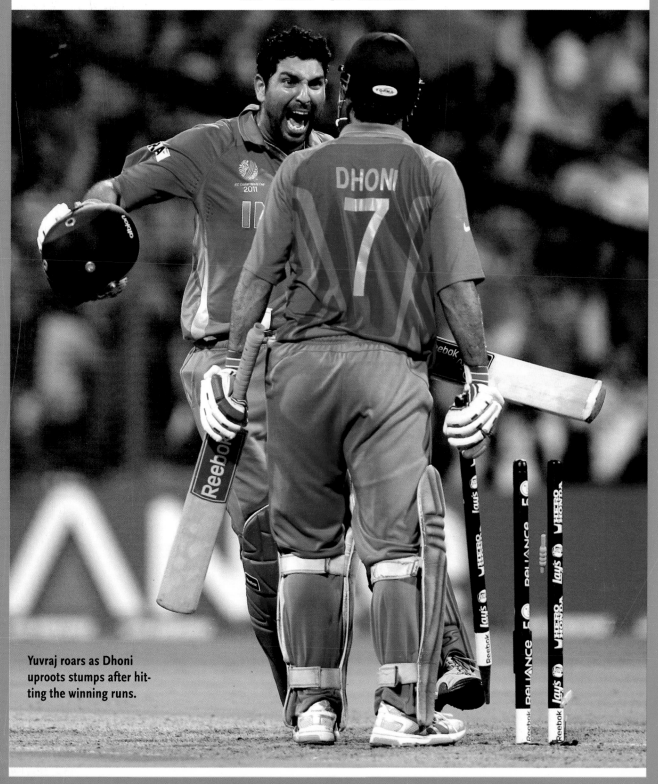

Yuvraj roars as Dhoni uproots stumps after hitting the winning runs.

Vs Sri Lanka

Dhoni and lead India to World

Turning Point

India's successful run chase could not have been possible without the effort of Gautam Gambhir, who missed out on his ton by three runs and skipper Mahendra Singh Dhoni, who scored an unbeaten 91 to signal his comeback to form.

However, the turning point was the third wicket 83-run stand between Virat Kohli and Gautam Gambhir.

After putting 274 runs on board, Sri Lanka paceman Lasith Malinga had scalped Virender Sehwag and Sachin Tendulkar early and the Lankans were going gung-ho, that's when Kohli and Gambhir arrived. They batted with gusto to change the face of the game.

Man-of-the-Match

India skipper Mahendra Singh Dhoni won the MoM award for his unbeaten 91.

Indian players celebrate the biggest win of their lives.

Gambhir
Cup glory

A brilliant 97 from Gautam Gambhir and a masterclass unbeaten 91 from skipper MS Dhoni saw India becoming the first host nation to win a World Cup and recapture the crown that Kapil Dev and his men first lifted at Lord's in 1983. The win also saw the home team pulling off the highest run-chase ever achieved in a World Cup final.

Against a triumphant backdrop at the Wankhede Stadium, victory was sealed by six wickets with 10 balls to spare, as Dhoni - who had promoted himself to No. 5 to heap extra lashings of responsibility onto his own shoulders - rushed through the gears as the victory target drew nearer. With 15 required from 17 balls, he flicked Sri Lanka's only true threat, Lasith Malinga, through midwicket for consecutive boundaries, before smoking Nuwan Kulasekara over long-on to finish on 91 not out from 79 balls, and spark the most delirious scenes of celebration ever seen on the subcontinent. However, the final margin did little justice to the tussle that had preceded it. Even the toss ended up being disputed, as Kumar Sangakkara's initial call was drowned out by the crowd, but it was the ebb and flow of Zaheer Khan's day that epitomised the fluctuations of a compelling contest. Zaheer opened his account with three consecutive maidens and the scalp of Upul Tharanga in a peerless spell of 5-3-6-1, only to be clobbered for 17 and 18 runs in his ninth and tenth overs, as Sri Lanka monstered 63 runs in the batting powerplay to post an imposing 274 for 6.

And India's day got much worse before the team's fortunes began to inch upwards. Virender Sehwag had hit a boundary from the

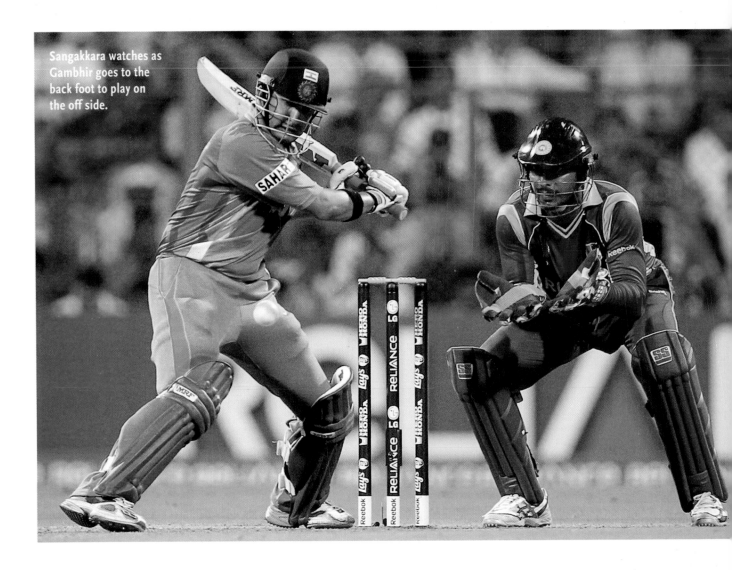

Sangakkara watches as Gambhir goes to the back foot to play on the off side.

Gambhir and Virat Kohli epitomise a generation that does not easily accept defeat.

first ball of six of India's previous eight innings in the tournament, but this time Malinga's slingers dealt him a second-ball duck, as he skidded a full delivery into his back pad. And then Sachin Tendulkar, for whom the script had seemingly been written, was drawn into a loose drive by a fast Malinga outswinger, having set the stadium on standby for instant history with 18 sumptuously accumulated runs from his first 12 deliveries.

At 31 for 2 in the seventh over, India were struggling to keep their toehold in the contest, and it was all too much for a faithless few in the crowd who turned their backs and set off for home. But Gambhir and Virat Kohli epitomise a generation that does not easily accept defeat, and their third-wicket stand of 83 laid the foundations for an epic turnaround. The prospect of a seam-friendly surface, allied to the grievous loss of Angelo Mathews to a thigh strain, had tempted Sri Lanka into four key changes to the team that had triumphed over New Zealand in Colombo, and with Muttiah Muralitharan lacking bite in the final wicket-less appearance of his 19-year career, Malinga alone could not carry the day.

The hard-hitting of Nuwan Kulasekara and Thisara Perera had been instrumental in hoisting Sri Lanka's total to such heights, but in their primary role as front-line seamers they lacked menace and were all too easy to squeeze as 119 runs came from their combined allocation of 17.2 overs. The newcomer to the squad, Suraj Randiv, caused a moment of alarm with his high-kicking offspin when Gambhir, on 30, was dropped by a diving

Gambhir & Dhoni were involved in a crucial partnership.

Kulasekara at long-off, but as the innings progressed, his lack of guile proved costly. The decision to omit both Ajantha Mendis and Rangana Herath, whose combined efforts had been so effective against England and New Zealand, is one that will haunt Sri Lanka for years to come.

But this was a victory that still had to be grasped, and India found the men who were willing to do so. The 22-year-old Kohli, who was greeted with a stern word of encouragement as he replaced the outgoing Tendulkar, showed all the mettle for the big occasion as he eased along to 35 from 49 balls before falling to an outstanding return catch by Tillakaratne Dilshan, who dived full-length across the crease to intercept a leading edge. But it was Gambhir and Dhoni to whom the ultimate duty fell. Their 109-run stand was the highest by an Indian pairing in three World Cup final appearances, and even when Gambhir gave away the chance for an unforgettable century with a tired charge and slash at Perera, the result was no longer in doubt.

Gambhir struck nine fours in a 122-ball statement of indomitability, and both he and Dhoni required treatment for stiff backs as the sapping Mumbai heat took its toll. Dhoni at one stage looked so immobile that a precautionary retirement seemed the only logical response, but after some harsh work from the physio he resumed his stance and responded with another trademark filleting of the extra cover boundary, an area in which he scored six

It was Gambhir and Dhoni to whom the ultimate duty fell.

of his eight fours - three of which helped to blunt Murali's attacking instincts.

Both teams contained numerous veterans of World Cup final defeat, with no fewer than five Indians still remaining from the team that lost to Australia back in 2003, and as a consequence this was a match thick with performances that spoke of the wisdom of experience. Though each of the previous five centuries in finals had gone on to lift the trophy, as well as seven of the nine teams that had had the chance to bat first, Jayawardene had the misfortune to become an exception to both rules. His stunning 103 not out from 88 balls was proof that finesse has as much of a place at this level as brutality, but ultimately it was not enough to deny India their destiny.

Four years ago at Sabina Park, Jayawardene produced a supreme century against New Zealand to carry his side to their second World Cup final, but this was an innings of even more exquisite application. He came to the crease with his side under the cosh at 60 for 2 in the 17th over, having been throttled by Zaheer's supreme new-ball spell. But he responded with a tempo that scarcely wavered from a run a ball, until with Kulasekera for company, he opened his shoulders to power through to his hundred from 84 balls.

For an occasion of this magnitude, cool heads were the order of the day, and though his final figures did not show it, no-one was cooler in the opening exchanges than Zaheer. On his watch, Sri Lanka were limited to 31 for 1 in their mandatory powerplay, their lowest ten-over score of the tournament, and the hapless Tharanga was restricted to two runs

This was a victory that still had to be grasped, and India found the men who were willing to do so.

MS Dhoni slaps one through the off side.

from 20 balls before snicking to Sehwag at slip, whose sharp low take epitomised a fielding effort that was rarely less than totally committed. Then, when he returned in the 37th over, Zaheer deceived Chamara Kapugedera with a beautiful slower ball that was driven to short cover, on route to equalling Shahid Afridi as the tournament's leading wicket-taker, with 21.

And yet, the speed with which his figures were vandalised was astounding. Though each of Jayawardene's 13 fours was a classy stroke in its own right, none was better than the last of them, an inside-out cover-drive to one of Zaheer's trademark outswinging yorkers, as he premeditated the late movement and filleted the ring of fielders on the off-side. The outright acceleration came from the other end, however, where Kulasekera made 32 from 30 balls before his sacrificial run-out led to a pat of gratitude from Jayawardene as they parted. And then, by the time Perera, who made 22 from nine balls, had sealed his onslaught with a dismissive thump for six over midwicket, the decibel levels in the Wankhede had plummeted.

But run by run, over by over, minute by minute, India picked themselves up, dusted themselves down, and turned the screw on Sri Lanka with a determination that a lesser group of men could not have begun to muster, amid the sure knowledge that several billion countrymen were investing all their hopes in their actions. And though he himself played just a walk-on part in the wider drama, it was Tendulkar who was chaired from the field as the celebrations began in earnest. "He's carried the burden of our nation for 21 years," said the youngster Kohli. "It was time to carry him on our shoulders today." 😄

Dhoni gave the final touch and ended confusion about world cup winner.

The champions celebrate with the World Cup trophy.

It's time to Cel

ebrate

Bhajji acknowledges the cheers from fans.

Sachin waves the Indian flag in triumph.

All for the sake of tri-color.

From top: It's disco time for Yuvi & Co.

Sachin takes a victory lap along with daughter Sara & son Arjun.

From top: Mahi showing the power of his gold medal.

Coach Gary Kirsten is carried around the ground.

Tears of elation for Yuvi as he is surrounded by team-mates.

M S DHONI

Didn't know how to celebrate win

Q On why he didn't go wild after the win.

Emotions were running very high. As soon as I hit the six, I was almost half-way down the pitch and I thought I would grab the stumps at the non-striker's end as souvenirs. But then I saw Yuvraj standing there and I was afraid he will grab that stump. I then told myself, forget hugging Yuvraj, let me grab a stump first. That confusion made me stand still in the middle of the pitch.

Q On the crowd support at the Wankhede.

Despite losing the wickets of Virender Sehwag and SachinTendulkar, the crowd still applauded every single run as if it was a boundary. I must say the crowd at all the venues supported us throughout the tournament.

Q On team's unity.

It was nearly eighteen months ago when the team set winning the World Cup as its goal. We wanted to win this for each other and for the nation. Everything that we were doing was keeping the World Cup in mind. It was a challenge to ensure that

our best player's didn't get injured before the World Cup. And we managed it. The format also helped us to peak at the right time. There were a lot of league games and that allowed us to field all combinations and arrive with our best team in the knockouts.

Q On his tremendous success as the leader.

I think I am very lucky. And all the guys have responded well to my leadership. 😊

Crowd at all the venues supported us through out the tournament.

All-round Hero: Yuvraj Singh

The Masterstroke for India's Greatness

The role of Yuvraj Singh as a part time bowler worked wonders for India.

Yuvraj Singh's heroics with the bat in the ICC Cricket World Cup 2011 have once again reiterated that he is a match winner and particularly one who reserves his best for the big match situations. On Yuvraj's broad and sturdy shoulders, India have been able to grow stronger and stronger in the tournament, eventually peaking at the right moment to be crowned the ICC Cricket World Cup 2011 champions.

If one were to look back on Yuvraj Singh in the tournament, four Man of the Match awards are indicative of the fact that of the nine matches that India played on the road to becoming champions, Yuvraj Singh has been outstanding and more poignantly an all rounder, but more specifically as a batsman when India needed a man for the crisis.

In the match against Ireland, Yuvraj Singh's half century was mature, steady and secured India a win when blushes seemed around the corner. His belligerence was evident in a contrasting half century against England. The century against the West Indies in a match where India needed to re-establish their ascendancy going into the knock out phase of the tournament proved pivotal as it helped India dominate the erratic West Indies in the second half of the match.

Against Australia, Yuvraj Singh was simply sublime in his knock of fifty-seven runs as he took India past the three time champions. That innings essayed in many ways the character of Yuvraj Singh as a bold, larger-than-life, highly gifted but determined tough cricketer at the crease, made for the stage in a battle between giants, past and present.

It takes tremendous self belief to stomp down the voice of doubt and defeat and Yuvraj Singh has had plenty of that in the past year as he battled injuries intermittently and fell out of favour thereafter. Yuvraj Singh spoke of those moments of doubt. But

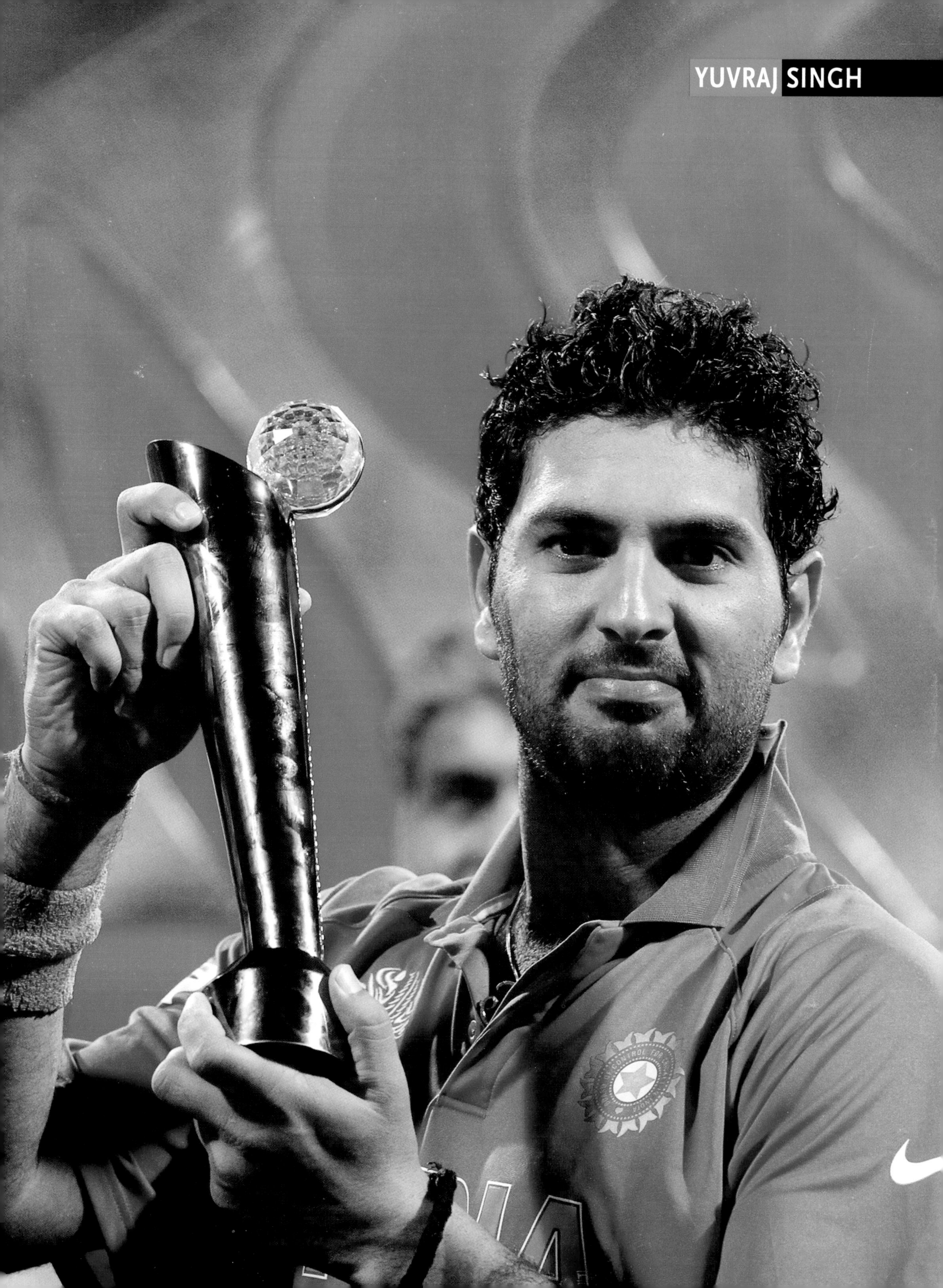

it is evident that the lion hearted all rounder had more mettle than people gave him credit for to come back in a fashion that has seen him carve the role of a finisher when India needed to cross the finish line with a mature head, play the role of the senior cricketer steering the team away from a precipitous position when wickets fell cheaply and completely the role of providing a firewall for teams looking to capitalize on any chinks in India's armour.

With an average of 90.50 from nine matches with a strike rate of 86.19, he is only marginally behind Gautam Gambhir (393 runs) and Virender Sehwag (380 runs) on the top run scorers for India in the ICC Cricket World Cup 2011 with 362 runs. His average though is the most important statistic because he is by far the best batsman of the tournament on that statistic alone. Combined with his all round contributions, Yuvraj Singh paints a pretty formidable picture all on his own.

Yuvraj Singh's stature with the bat has been re-established once more with his exceptional consistency during the ICC Cricket World Cup 2011.

To his credit, numbers alone do not do him justice. Instead when one looks back on the tough year he has had preceding the ICC Cricket World Cup 2011, his contribution to team India magnitude many more times that what his efforts seem worthy in only the context of the tournament. Yuvraj Singh fought a year when his place was considered under threat from the younger brat pack, but he came back in such strong fashion that it is not hard to see why the Indian captain, Mahendra Singh Dhoni, looked at class in Yuvraj Singh's batting and not his current form when he picked him up as the right hand senior man to guide India in South Africa in the run up to the ICC Cricket World Cup 2011. It was the partnership between Dhoni and Yuvraj Singh in the end that allowed India to keep their faith intact, and

composure cool as India went in for the final runs to beat Sri Lanka in a tense finish to the final. Complete contrast to the determination at the crease where no emotions was allowed a brief let up was when an emotional Yuvraj Singh broke down when the final runs were hit. It was be the enduring image of what it means to a sportsman to surpass overwhelming odds and make a country of a billion people proud.

It is perhaps why Yuvraj Singh is the more celebrated batsman in India's line up in light of this trophy simply because his story of a year that was described as his worst in a decade in international cricket to bounce back to be India's chief protagonist in lifting the trophy in twenty-eight years is the stuff of legends. The only thing more impressive than Yuvraj Singh's lofted shots for six is his ability to stamp his indelible authority on the game, or as in this case, the ICC Cricket World Cup 2011.

The Game Changer

Yuvraj Singh's stature with the bat has been reestablished once more with his exceptional consistency during the ICC Cricket World Cup 2011. But in his role as a part time bowler, Yuvraj Singh has been exceptional, doing the dynamic job not only as an all

Yuvraj Singh roars after taking India to victory against Australia.

Yuvi acknowledges the cheers after scoring his 13th ODI ton.

Yuvraj lets out a victory cry.

rounder but also, more than making up for the chinks in India's armour to become the chief architect of India's success in the ICC Cricket World Cup 2011.

Yuvraj Singh's all round contributions make him the complete package and the critical factor in India's stupendous victory since 1983. After battling wrist and finger injuries, Yuvraj Singh was back at his familiar point position, leading the battle cry with the young guards also kept on their feet and matched for agility by a player who struggled the year before to recapture his image as an electrifying fielder and also, a live wire in the field to keep the team sharp on their toes.

Gary Kirsten, India's outgoing coach, even acknowledged as much in one of his interviews following the ICC Cricket World

Cup 2011 of the role of Yuvraj Singh as also, the hard work and time the latter put in towards getting back on his own feet. Kirsten was all praise for Yuvraj Singh for getting into the thick of things six months prior to the commencement of the ICC Cricket World Cup 2011 and working on his fitness, fielding and agility in the field with the aid of the support staff. Kirsten was clearly impressed that one of the lynchpins of modern Indian cricket was looking beyond a difficult year and looking

India were ecstatic after Yuvraj's dismissal of Michael Clarke.

beyond making amends to actually take a huge responsibility on his shoulders as far as India's goals were concerned.

Make no mistake. Yuvraj Singh the batsman was invaluable. But Yuvraj Singh, the bowler, was just as priceless for India's cause. To finish up as the second leading wicket taker for India with fifteen wickets to tournament leader, Zaheer Khan, on twenty-one wickets, is no mean feat. At a time when India's designated spinners, Harbhajan Singh and Piyush Chawla, were struggling to extract opponents, Yuvraj Singh was superior by leaps and bounds in that he was able to flummox the batsmen not necessarily with spin but also, with guile and variation in pace. And the

> Yuvraj Singh the batsman was invaluable. Yuvraj Singh, the bowler, was just as priceless for India's cause.

rewards were so consistent that Yuvraj Singh was reckoned as much as India's frontline bowler in their strategic planning at one point, evident in that Yuvraj was getting almost the full allotment overs in the game.

Yuvraj Singh's prowess with the ball can never again be underestimated. Always an interesting alternative option for the captain, Yuvraj Singh bowled himself into cricket history when he became the first cricketer in World Cup history to take five wickets in a match and also, score a half century. He did it in the game against Ireland, where India needed a steady hand with the bat but also, someone who could stop the

Yuvi roars after taking his first five-wicket haul.

Yuvraj Singh was Mahendra Singh Dhoni's go-to man and he delivered almost every time when the captain turned to him.

sticky Irish team who simply refused to believe they did not belong higher up on the rungs in international cricket.

Yuvraj Singh was Mahendra Singh Dhoni's go-to man and he delivered almost every time when the captain turned to him. Consistently picking up a couple of vital wickets to disturb the calm in the opposition dressing room, Yuvraj Singh became the nightmare of almost every team that India faced, and sometimes it did not even matter that Yuvraj Singh did not have anything to do with the bat. Yuvraj Singh with the ball posed a bigger threat on the day than any of India's second line of pace attack or even India's leading spin king, Harbhajan Singh.

That speaks volumes of the responsibility that Yuvraj Singh took on at a time when India could have been exposed for their inability to curtail the opposition enough to secure wins without another specialist bowler to turn to. Dhoni's sometimes self admitted gambles to go with pace did not handicap him severely for spin because Yuvraj Singh filled in the role beautifully.

Etching himself into the plans to cover India's base from all angles, Yuvraj Singh was mesmerizing with the ball as he was with his majestic shot making with the bat. Bowling seventy-five overs over nine matches makes him virtually one of India's chief bowlers in their plot lines. This, however, was not entirely planned. But when plan A did not surface in India's bowling attack, Yuvraj Singh became the Plan B that played out so seamlessly that it never seemed as if India were caught off guard by the lack of bowling resources to back up Zaheer Khan's stealer efforts with the ball. The dynamism of Yuvraj Singh was always evident. But coming to the fore as it did in fashioning India's victory, one would be forgiven for thinking that India's success depended on one man's ability turn his arm over, game after game, steering situations to India's advantage time and again. 🏏

It's the most important trophy of my life

Q On Sir Vivian Richards comment just before the World cup that your style reminded him of his own batting?

It's a huge compliment for me when someone like Sir Viv thinks this about me. One feels really nice. There could not have been a better motivation just before the mega-event. And, when one delivers on such high expectations, it's immensely satisfying.

Q On the never-seen-before kind of celebration across the country after the triumph.

I saw VIPs like Madam Sonia Gandhi celebrating the win with common men on the streets. I heard that superstars like Mr Amitabh Bachchan and Mr Shahrukh Khan were celebrating like a cricket fan. It looked like the entire nation has won the cup. Everyone wished for us and thankfully we lived up to the expectations.

Q On the most important person behind his all-round success.

Sachin Tendulkar. No doubt about that. People kept asking me about the name of the person who transformed my success as an all-rounder, and I just said that I would reveal the name only after

the World Cup. Sachin is the man. I didn't name him during the tournament because I wanted to play for him. I have a special bond with him. We all had tears in our eyes when the best moment of our career arrived. I have never seen everyone crying with happiness in the dressing room.

On the player of the tournament trophy.
Yes, it is the most important trophy of my life. More than anything else, it helped me to fulfill the dream of the great Sachin Tendulkar. It is the most prized possession for sure.

On being two different Yuvraj, on and off the field.
I am a different person on and off the field. I may look aggressive on field but am quite soft off the field. I easily forgive my enemies when they say sorry. I hug them immediately and don't hold any grudge against anyone. I don't have double standards in life. I talk straight.

On Ricky Ponting's comment that he never saw a more determined Yuvi after the quarter final game.
Definitely. The innings against the Australians was the turning point for me. I thought it gave us the momentum, as the Aussies were the team to beat, seeing their extraordi-

nary run in the last 3 World Cups.

On whether it was only appropriate that he and Dhoni were batting when the winning run was being scored.
Surely. We support each other like a family does to its members. MS is a special player. He always rises to the big occasion. People were talking about his lack of runs and see how he took the responsibility in the finals. As batting partners, we handle crunch situations well while chatting up in the middle.

On Zaheer Khan's silent and yet unforgettable contribution.
He has been a warrior for this team India. Whenever we needed wicket, he was always there. Be it new ball or be it old ball, Zaheer is one of the architects of this stupendous victory.

On his best bowling moment.
My 5 wicket haul against Ireland. I may get many hundreds more but am not sure about another 5 wicket haul in future!

On his best moment of the World Cup.
There are so many. MS's last ball six, Raina's composure against Australia and of course Sachin's batting against Pakistan, Viru's assault on the new balls as well. 😊

Everyone wished for us and thankfully we lived up to the expectations.

Batting Hero: Sachin Tendulkar

The Dreamer Imparts Lesson in Grit, Glory and Never Giving Up

Sachin
Tendulkar
is now one
of the chief
protagonists
to have
given the
nation more
than the
dream of the
World Cup.

I t is hard to imagine that Sachin Tendulkar was still a genius in the making when the dream of winning the World Cup was first spawn in his mind. Yet incredible determination, self belief beyond comprehension, deep seated hunger, innumerable hours of toil and endurance of pain, and never giving up his dream meant that twenty-eight years later Sachin Ramesh Tendulkar is now one of the chief protagonists to have given the nation more than the dream of the World Cup. He has brought home the trophy – only the second time in India's cricket history - by his own premeditated design.

The Ultimate Dream catcher

If there was ever a need to validate Sachin Tendulkar as the game's most imposing run getter, he amplified it in the 18,000th run he scored in the quarterfinal match against Australia in a crucial half century. That he is a colossal genius was emphasized as he moved to ninety-nine international centuries, and almost had his hundredth in the semi final match against Pakistan when he notched up eighty-five runs, built without being fazed by the fact that fortune had a role to play in a slightly more flawed performance on the day. It showed him as mortal though not associating him with the word 'mere' by any stretch of the imagination.

Instrumental in India's second World Cup victory, Tendulkar showed the genius of his talent and the grit of his bat in the ICC Cricket World Cup 2011 as he laid out the foundation for India to not only strive but actually accomplish what was never done by any team in the history of the World Cup – win the trophy on home soil.

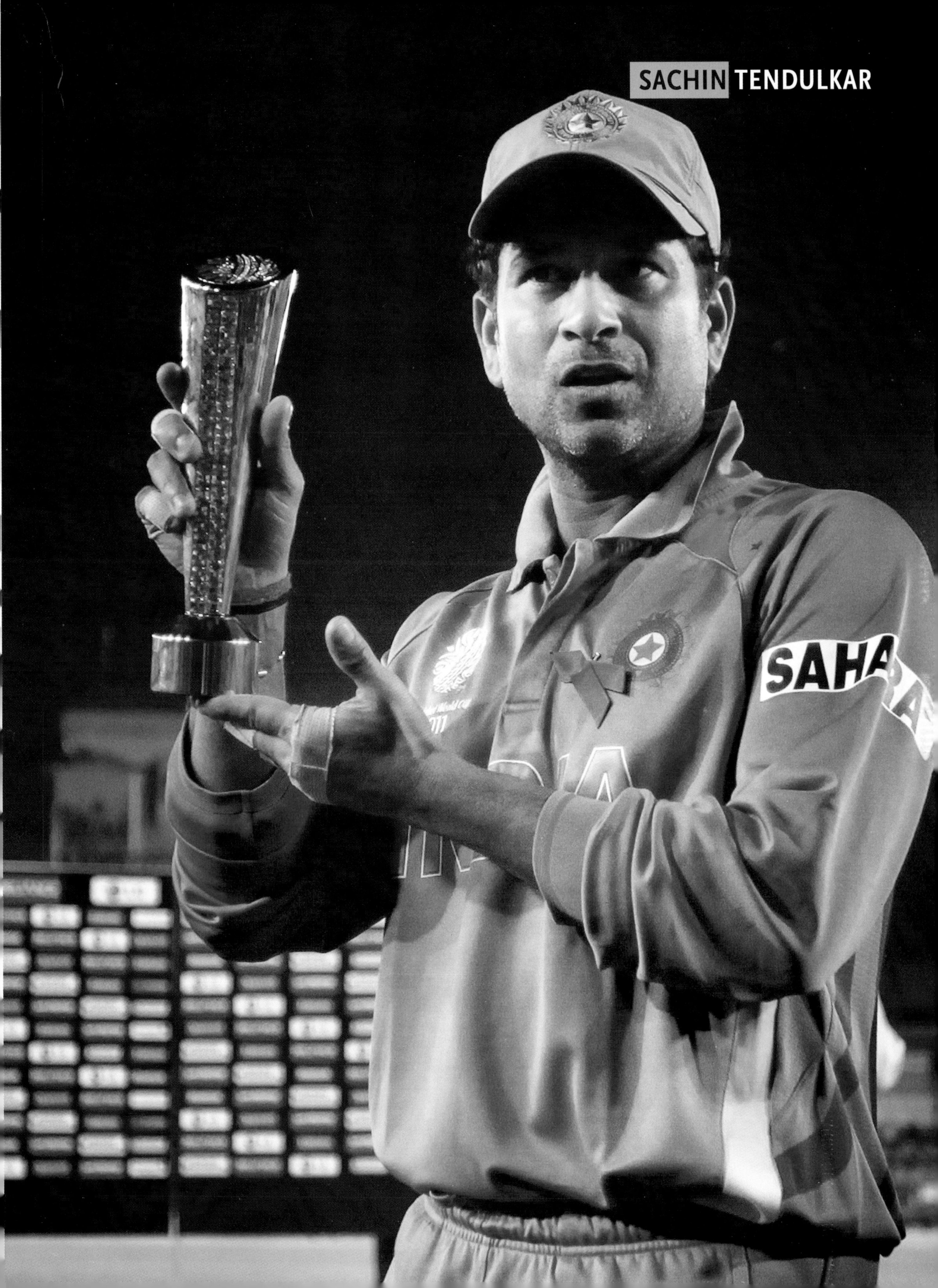

Twenty-one years would seem almost too long to hold on to the dream that first stirred his heart. Not to Sachin Tendulkar as he crossed that magnificent milestone of his professional cricket playing years. He made the World Cup dream his own much before when as a ten year old, impressionable budding cricketer, he witnessed Kapil Dev's Indian cricket team lift the World Cup back in 1983, defying odds, talent and the might of the West Indies.

If that win lifted the spirits of a nation, it inspired a whole new generation to aspire to live up to those astounding accomplishments. But to Tendulkar, it was more than an aspiration. It became the mission statement of his life. It took six World Cup edition appearances, unwavering belief even in the midst of despair and determination from deep within that saw him not only rise above his personal battles within his cricket career but also, rise above the fallibility that trailed Indian cricket

Two important back to back half centuries followed in the knock stages that pivoted India into the exalted position of playing their third Cricket World Cup final.

teams in the past to land at the very pinnacle of the sport.

Willow wielder of the genius kind
On the verge of 18,000 ODI runs, and ninety-seven international centuries, one would thought Tendulkar would be content to sit on his laurels that could outweigh the stigma of India never having won the World Cup in his time. But to Tendulkar, the flame that kindled his heart in 1983 became a burning desire even in the midst of a bushfire that surrounded the Indian cricket team following their suffocating and humiliating exit in the 2007 edition.

But by his own admission, 2007 was one of the low points in his career. However, where most would have thrown in the towel, Tendulkar put the negativity of being written off aside and instead, worked even harder to carry that dream forward for another four years, knowing that this was his one chance to do it in front of the home crowds. Runs replaced injuries, resolve replaced fervour and individual milestones took second seat to rallying around spirit within the team to rise to their potential.

There was every danger of the Indian cricket team being suffocated by the home pressure and Tendulkar himself was in danger of being distracted by the public euphoria and media hype about the anticipation of the hundred international centuries. However, Tendulkar has not achieved the kind of unprecedented attention and adulation for nothing. Not only did he not lose sight of the bigger team goal that he nourished more, knowing plausibly at the back of his mind that personal milestones would follow in time, but also, refused to be clouded by the Indian players' bold declarations of wanting to win the World Cup for Sachin Tendulkar. To him, winning the

World Cup for India was his mission as much as it was for every other member of the Indian squad, his sense of responsibility to the realization much greater in light of his lifelong ambition.

A couple of centuries en route failed to bring home the points as India approached the knock out stages of the tournament and it was not for want of Tendulkar's efforts. Two important back to back half centuries followed in the knock stages that pivoted India into the exalted position of playing their third Cricket World Cup final. While his own cricket records were being broken, Tendulkar's most prized innings in the ICC Cricket World Cup 2011 would have to arguably be the eighty-five runs he scored against Pakistan in a highly charged semi final contest in Mohali.

Skeptics would say Tendulkar led a charmed life in India's innings. But champions are those who ride out the hurdles and come through when it re-

Sachin about to lift the ball for a six on his way to a century against England.

ally counts. Sachin Tendulkar saw purpose when others saw leverage lost on the part of Pakistan through their own sloppy efforts in the field. Refusing to succumb to the notion that things were not going as he would have planned, Tendulkar dug in his heels and never looked back. Eighty-five runs were seen as fifteen short of what would have been his hundredth international century. To Sachin Tendulkar, those eighty-five runs perhaps epitomize his efforts for India to crown his World Cup efforts.

Tendulkar incidentally was also the highest run getter for India in the tournament, notching up 482 runs at an impressive average of 53.55, second only to Sri Lanka's Tillakaratne Dilshan who scored eighteen runs more than him. In scoring the runs, he pulled away even further from the pack of batsmen in that he crossed 18,000 ODI runs, pegging back the now retired Sanath Jayasuriya at 13,428 runs and certainly widening the gap between himself and Ricky Ponting who stands on 13, 406 runs. The gargantuan appetite of the man for the game was not only evident in the number of runs that he has kept on adding to the tally but also, in the manner in which he never lost sight of the big picture.

Always holding onto the Dream

Sachin Tendulkar never stopped nurturing the dream. Suffice it to say, Tendulkar saw a golden opportunity when four years ago, the nation only saw despair in tattered dreams. Written off as past his best-by date, Sachin Tendulkar's determination only grew fiercer. Count on Tendulkar to breathe life into them, this time with more tenacity and brilliance that perhaps ever witnessed before.

Tendulkar saw method where others saw mayhem. His mission was simple and flawless. With the ambition actively living and breathing in his heart as it had when under the tutelage of his coach, Ramakant Achrekar and in the environs of Shivaji Park in Mumbai, Sachin Tendulkar went into the ICC Cricket World Cup 2011, defying those who extolled him speculating of his retirement at the end of the last edition, with

the single minded purpose of bringing home glory once more, this time on home soil.

Tendulkar defied age and reflex notions as he accelerated in the period between the last ICC Cricket World Cup in 2007 and the next, the ICC Cricket World Cup 2011. His vision never seemed better, his coordination smoother than ever, taking profligacy out of the equation and working prolifically on his game but simultaneously instilling the dream of the World Cup and the dedication required in the younger members of the squad. While Tendulkar elevated his own goals, he helped mentor those in the team to the point where the reliance on Tendulkar

Sachin goes after a short ball.

seems to have reduced on the cricket field when India bats. But when viewed closely, Dhoni and his wards are often waxing eloquently of working in the slipstream of the batting maestro who happens to be the world's leading run scorer. That his very presence in the team adds just a tremendous strength is immense although not surprising.

Team man to the core, Tendulkar would be the first to acknowledge that it was the cohesive team efforts that paved the way for the realization of a long nurtured dream. But it is hard to imagine that any cricketer worth his name worked harder than the man himself or put more pressure and onus on himself to lead the way majestically

Sachin Tendulkar's monumental efforts in the sport: Dreams never die; dreamers never fade.

with the bat in hand. It could not have been easy to make such an emphatic comeback following the kind of injuries Tendulkar has had to endure in his time and for a man whose personal achievements could have left him complacent, it was the larger team goal he held close to his heart that motivated him to lead by example. The rub off on the generations privileged to play with him should keep

India in good stead beyond the World Cup.

At an age where winning the World Cup would be considered too ambitious to even imagine, to Sachin Tendulkar, it was the realization of his life's ambition, the most prominent one anyway. True to Tendulkar's style, he emphasized through his own example that the stronger the will, the fiercer the determination with diligence to boot, no goal is beyond the realm of the possible.

That was the message Sachin Tendulkar sent out once more after India won the ICC Cricket World Cup 2011. If his eyes lit up at the thought of India winning the World Cup before, the sparkle in his eye will carry forth that important life lesson: never give up in life, he said. One would like to add in light of Sachin Tendulkar's monumental efforts in the sport: Dreams never die; dreamers never fade. 😊

Sachin slashes one through covers.

It was an extremely emotional moment

Q On teammates wanting to win the World Cup for him.

That all the teammates wanted to win this World Cup for me, was very touching and moving. And, also within the team, we were playing for each other and above all, playing for the nation. We wanted to win this for the Indian team and also for all the well-wishers of this country.

Q On the kind of responsibility and pressure on him during the World Cup.

I don't think that only senior cricketers have the responsibility. When a 15-member squad is picked, then all players have the responsibility. Different matches see different responsibilities and each player has equal responsibility.

Q On him motivating youngsters throughout the tournament.

It was my dream to win the World Cup and so was it for the others. For that, we needed proper planning and it was very important to know from which way the team had to move forward to reach their goals. At different stages, not only me, but I have seen members of the team encouraging someone. We advised each other on how to get better and how our performances could be

improved. When the big moment came, all players were charged up and everybody knew how important this moment will be in their career. Everybody was prepared and all were calm, we were not thinking about the pressure, were not thinking about expectations. We were just thinking about our process and we were just thinking about how we will give our best in the final.

Q On the kind of pressure the team had this time, especially after the first round exit during the 2007 World Cup in West Indies.

I don't think there was more pressure. Pressure is always there on all the players. There was pressure of my own expectations. I wanted to do something special this time. I won't call it pressure, but it was preparation. As an individual, we think of giving our best every time. If any bowler fails one day, then we hope that another bowler comes out and takes wickets. We were just thinking as individuals. How can all players give their best? It's all team effort. If you look, there will be times when one batsman has not scored while the other has. We just try to cover other's failure on that day, so that when you fail some other day, other individuals will try to cover up.

Q On preparations for that particular moment.

Frankly speaking, we were just not thinking about it. We planned things, but nobody was thinking of lifting the trophy. Obviously, at the back of our minds, we wanted to do it. We wanted to follow the process, wanted to first finish the game, win it and then go for the trophy. In our minds, it was about how well we can restrict them to whatever minimum possible total and then chase it and then think about the trophy. It happened when we were not even thinking about lifting the trophy before the match. Yes, we all wanted to do that but there was a process we had on how to get there and we were just focusing on it.

Q On Mahendra Singh Dhoni as a captain.

I think he is a fabulous captain. He stayed calm, patient and at the same time, very clever and alert. Situational awareness has been his great strength and obviously, to know what every individual likes and dislikes is important. And he has been at it throughout the tournament. I think he is the best captain under whom I have ever played.

Q On the victory lap after the match...

It was an extremely emotional moment. I want to thank my teammates for that gesture. I was not expecting all that, I was taken by surprise. What a way to end the World Cup. It was an overwhelming experience.

It was my dream to win the World Cup and so was it for the others.

Zaheer
Khan was
the single
bowling
powerhouse
in the ICC
Cricket
World Cup
2011.

Bowling Hero: Zaheer Khan

Zaheer Works World Cup Magic into India's Bowling Prowess

I ndia's victory in the ICC Cricket World Cup 2011 was made possible by three factors – the revival of the all rounder in Yuvraj Singh, the batting stronghold in Sachin Tendulkar and the single bowling powerhouse in Zaheer Khan. It would not be unfair to say that it was the latter that stood out given that the odds in India's favour as far as their bowling resources were concerned which also were not looking optimistic at the start of the competition.

Bulking up on responsibility

At the start of the ICC Cricket World Cup 2011, if there were apprehensions about the Indian cricket team, it revolved around two significant issues - the pressure of playing at home in front of gigantic crowds and the obvious delicate line of India's bowling attack. Zaheer Khan had already made his mark, quite clearly as the frontrunner, as the Indian spearhead. But what followed behind him left plenty of reason for concern.

Harbhajan Singh filled up the premier spinner's role where Zaheer Khan eased himself into the role of the versatile fast bowler. Thereafter, the decision between Ashish Nehra, Munaf Patel and even Sreesanth was seen as one of gamble for the Indian captain, Mahendra Singh Dhoni. In Munaf Patel, there was quiet, understated talent, but little confidence. In Ashish Nehra, there was erratic, inconsistent performance thrown in good measure. And in Sreesanth, the skipper had his hands full.

With the facts being what they were, heading into this tournament, there were concerns that Zaheer Khan would have not have a steady bowling partner to justify the adage that fast bowlers hunt in pairs. That could have proved to be India's weakest link because

while India's batting appeared lengthy, resolute, talented and determined, India's success in the discipline of bowling hinged greatly on Zaheer Khan taking on the bulk of the workload with a greater sense of responsibility than normally accorded in the limited frame of ten overs in a match.

Bowlers who can strike at the heart of the opposition are imperative to any team's success. Zaheer had a triple role to play and that was equally fairly apparent because India needed a strong opening bowling who could tear into a couple of wickets, bowl at the death with a miserly intention of conceding runs and even having to change track and bowl in the middle orders when the captain needed a breakthrough. There was only one name that could truly answer that call.

Behold the beauty in the beast of burden

Zaheer Khan was by far the best act to watch when India took to the field in the

Zaheer had a triple role to play and that was equally fairly apparent because India needed a strong opening bowling.

ICC Cricket World Cup 2011. Whether India were fielding first or second, the eyes remained fixated, for a majority of the innings, on two individuals – Mahendra Singh Dhoni, the Indian captain, in the way he marshaled his bowlers, and Zaheer Khan in whose hands, the ball took on a life of its own.

India owes it success in a sizable proportion to Zaheer Khan because it was the one area where India could have unraveled. If the stitches on the team stayed in place, it was because of what Zaheer Khan was able to extract out of the seam and pitch. There were plenty of moments in the course of the nine matches that India played where it seemed that their batting targets would be let down by the fragility in their bowling. But with the shadow of Zaheer Khan always lurking in the distance, India were able to pull back every time things threatened to get out of hand.

That there is no designated Indian bowler anywhere close to Zaheer Khan, barring the part time Yuvraj Singh who turned into a full time proposition for the captain, in the ICC Cricket World Cup 2011 is a fair indication of why the apprehensions were justified in the first place. But that these fears remained only that, fears which were overcome by India had a great deal to do with the fact that Zaheer Khan was stretching himself to full measure as he has had in the past four years or thereabouts for Indian cricket. The difference in his presence and absence from India's presence is akin to chalk and cheese.

Zaheer Khan was not only India's best bowler of the tournament but also, the highest wicket taker of the ICC Cricket World Cup 2011, sharing that spot with the Pakistan captain, Shahid Afridi, as if only to emphasize further why India were able to realize their dream of a second ICC Cricket World Cup trophy. With twenty-one wickets

at an average of 18.76, Zaheer Khan was able to provide India the fillip for their seemingly susceptible bowling resources, and gave Dhoni the upper hand even when the opposition chose to go hammer and tongs. Zaheer was effective in curtailing the opponents and also, in making sure that any slight error of judgement on the part of the skipper with regard to the composition of the team did not come back to haunt him.

Consolidating the Comeback

2011 presents a larger-than-life image of Zaheer Khan, making 2003 a faint rewind of Zaheer's past. The Indian spearhead not only turned his cricket fortunes around but also, changed the dynamics of team India, helping them pave the way to glory that was witnessed only once before in 1983. That he did it without qualms of what was a difficult World Cup final in 2003 speaks loudly of the gigantic leap of faith that has

Zaheer is ecstatic after breaking the partnership between Hussey & Ponting in the quarter finals.

been witnesses in the case of India's premier fast bowler.

In 2003, India had three promising left arm bowlers and India's pace attack seemed to brimming with talent and exuberance. And yet at the final hurdle, it was laid threadbare with inexperience, nerves and a bold onslaught from Australia. India's dream run to the final of the tournament ended rather tamely, taking away the closest opportunity India had had since 1983 to re-live the glory of the ICC Cricket World Cup.

Amongst the bowlers that suffered the ordeal, Zaheer Khan has had to live with the nightmare of a spell in that final against Australia. To make matters worse, Zaheer went through a critical phase where his commitment came into question following the World Cup. Stories soon began doing the rounds about Zaheer Khan's inability to maintain his focus, distractions that kept his talent at bay and his apparent lethargy to work hard enough on his own fitness. Things went quickly downhill for the fast bowler thereafter with injuries wrecking his comeback route back to the Indian cricket team.

Considered another Indian fast bowler consigned to the wilderness, Zaheer Khan staged a powerful fight back in 2006, witnessed not only in his tremendous rise in international circles quietly and quickly thereafter but also, in the pivotal role he played for India in the ICC Cricket World Cup 2011. A stronger, sharper, Zaheer Khan homed in on the target armed with variation, change of pace and ability to manipulate the ball, never entertaining a semblance of a doubt, and what followed was a steady derailment of plans for India's opponents.

Maturity, Intelligence – Zaheer's Strongest Traits

That Zaheer did not allow this vulnerability in the bowling attack to unduly give him cause for worry in light of the responsibility thrust upon him is already a tremendous transformation from the Zaheer Khan of 2003 who suffered the jangling of nerves against Australia to concede twenty-nine runs in his first three overs. In stark contrast, although Zaheer Khan did go for runs

in the end of the Sri Lankan innings, his first five over spell, in which three overs were maidens ,yielded just six runs, while taking the important wicket of Upul Tharanga. Gary Kirsten, the Indian coach, also acknowledged that spell as critical for India in restricting the resurgence of the Sri Lankans in the latter half of the innings in the final.

Zaheer's team mates acknowledge the degree of determination for the fast bowler to bounce back after a spate of injuries. Amongst the qualities acknowledged of the spearhead also include his superior knowledge of bowling on the unforgiving flat pitches of the sub continent. But it is a combination of factors that truly makes Zaheer Khan India's

Zaheer is overjoyed at dismissing Andrew Strauss - The game changing moment.

driving force.

Zaheer Khan is an enigma. Someone who know how to use the shine on the new ball wisely is also one of the rare, successful proponents of the art of swinging bowling, coming in rather handy for the skipper with the old ball as well. His shorter run up may suggest a diminishing pace, but the accuracy could not be faulted as also, his wicket taking ability which has been a huge factor in India clawing their way of situations that would have otherwise seemed to have slipped past their control. Zaheer Khan's intelligent bowling and fair assessment of the ploys playing in the minds of the opposition batsmen makes him a lethal proposition as India's opponents found out once more to their detriment in the ICC Cricket World Cup 2011.

The fact that there were several game changing moments when Zaheer took the ball signifies the times that the spearhead has been able to provide break-throughs that have proved decisive for India. It is hard to erase the memory of the yorker that undid the brilliance of the England captain. Andrew Strauss went all guns blazing in the chase of India's 338 in Bengaluru in the group phase. His

There were several game changing moments when Zaheer took the ball signifies the times.

150 runs were threatening to undo the work done by the batsmen when in the forty-third over, Zaheer Khan pulled the yorker out of his hat and struck yet again to bring India right back into the game.

The Indian skipper had his own turning point moment to mention when he referred to Zaheer Khan's dismissal of Devon Smith in the crucial final group match against the West Indies when it

success. In the quarterfinal match against Australia, Zaheer Khan bowled out Michael Hussey. It was a crucial wicket followed up by a clean caught and bowled dismissal of Cameron White in the larger scheme of things because it did not allow Australia the luxury to accelerate following Ricky Ponting's final heroic efforts as the Australian captain with a gritty century against his name.

But what makes Zaheer Khan's success even more spectacular is the attitude with which he went into the tournament and indeed, the final. While many would consider the experience of the ICC Cricket World Cup 2003 final a nightmarish episode for Zaheer Khan, Zaheer himself has spoken highly of one of the toughest moments in his career. Instead of looking down upon it as an unpleasant day at the office, Zaheer believes it owes it to that moment because it has been upward rising learning curve thereafter, giving him the tools with which to approach the game with greater knowledge and loads of experience. The confidence, the self assuredness, the presence of mind, the calmness and the discipline in harnessing of talent were a huge part of the class act that epitomizes Zaheer Khan in the ICC Cricket World Cup 2011. ✍

seemed that the West Indies were racing to a party. Once the might and majesty of Smith hit a brick wall with Zaheer Khan coming back for a second spell in Chennai, it was curtains for the team that strayed down the road of self destruction.

Another spectacular moment in the ICC Cricket World Cup 2011 has also been identified by Zaheer Khan himself as being pivotal in the context of India's

Zaheer Khan & Virat Kohli celebrate a wicket.

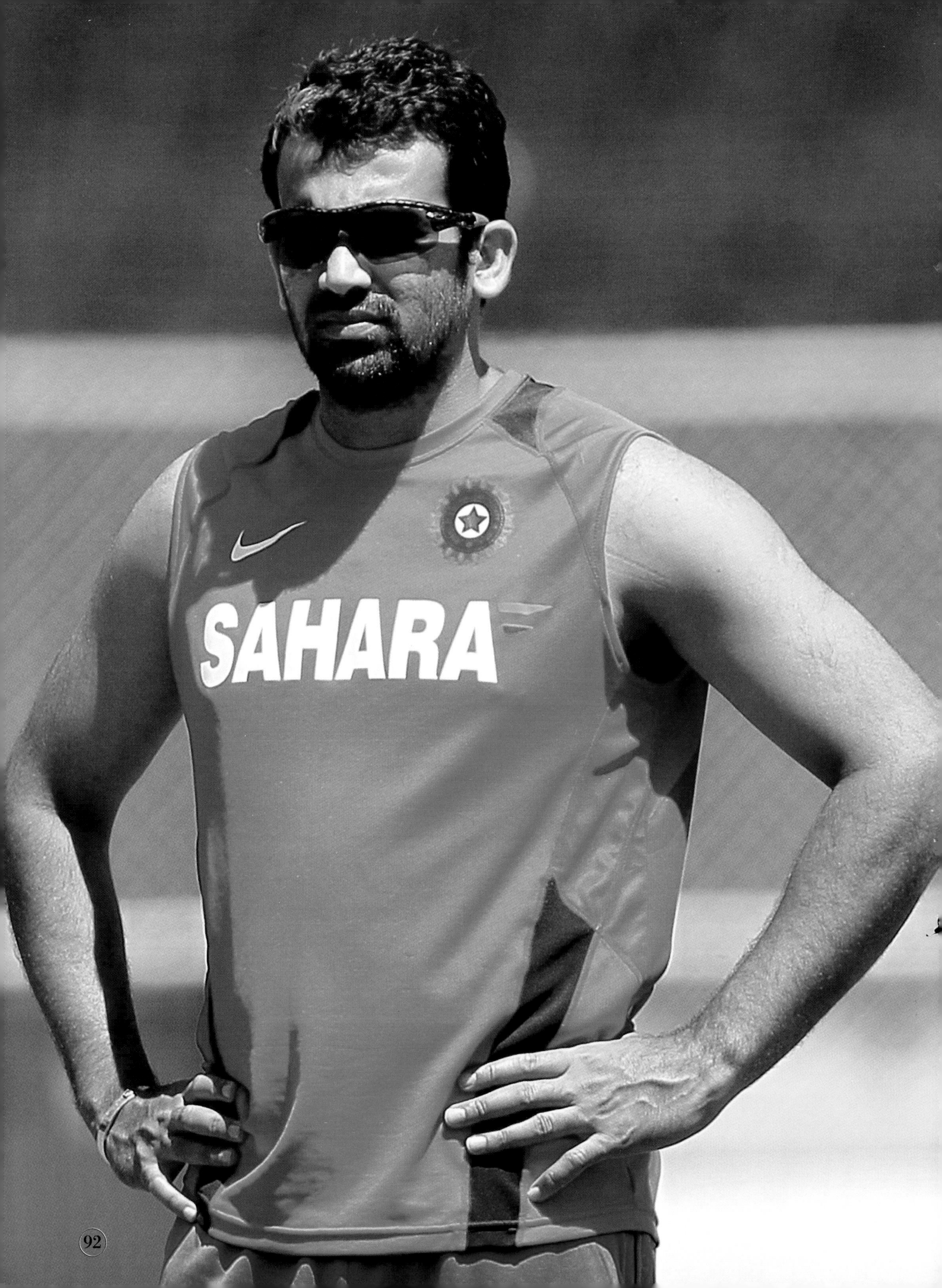
SAHARA

ZAHEER KHAN

Strauss and Hussey were my favourite World Cup wickets

Q On his best wicket of the World Cup.

Out of the 21 wickets which I took, Strauss and Hussey were my favourite World Cup wickets. Taking Andrew Strauss' wicket was a game-changing moment for us in Bangalore, it was a perfect yorker and something I'll always remember. Also in the quarter-final, taking Mike Hussey's wicket was really important – Ricky Ponting was playing well and it was important to break that partnership.

Q On the difference between 2003 and 2011 finals.

I'm glad that by playing in this World Cup I had the opportunity to change things from the past, but I do not regret 2003, it was a great learning experience, it meant I was more prepared for 2011 and ready to help India win this World Cup.

Q On coach Gary Kirsten.

Gary Kirsten is the only coach who has understood me well, given me the freedom to express myself, allowed me to get into my own space and given me the freedom to achieve.

Q On the winning moment.

We all knew when the ball hit the middle of the bat that MS Dhoni was going to be hitting a six to win the final. There's nothing like hitting a six to win the World Cup.

Q On the atmosphere in the dressing room after the win.

It was a special moment and it was a special day. To make history was in our hand. We supported each other and stayed united as a team. All the families were there in the dressing room. They were taking photos with the Cup. It was a great atmosphere there. ☺

Gary Kirsten is the only coach who has understood me well.

It's pouring millions for the Champions

Forget the World Cup trophy. It's raining cash and goodies too on our brave cricketers. It was a sweet victory that's being made sweeter with each passing day with the money raining on the Indian cricket team. Dhoni's men are being showered with goodies, cash prizes, cars, and even plots by different sections of the society.

MONEY TIME

The Board of Control for Cricket in India (BCCI) announced during the closing ceremony of the world cup that it was awarding 1 crore to each team member, 50 lakh to each of the support staff and 25 lakh to the selectors. However, seeing the stature of victory, BCCI later on increased their cash bonanza to 2 crore. Our politicians were also quick to follow suit in their generosity. Delhi chief minister Sheila Dikshit has announced 2 crore for MS Dhoni and 1 crore each for four Delhi players – Virender Sehwag, Gautam Gambhir, Virat Kohli and Ashish Nehra. Maharashtra CM Prithviraj Chavan too, announced awards of 1 crore each for Maharashtrian players Sachin Tendulkar and Zaheer Khan. Munaf Patel and Yusuf Pathan are set to receive 1 lakh each from the Gujarat government as part of the "Eklavya Puruskar", the highest sports award in the state. Even the Uttar Pradesh government is bestowing the Manyawar Kanshiram International Sports Award on Suresh Raina and Piyush Chawla, which carries a purse of one million rupees. The Punjab government has announced a cash award of 1crore each for Harbhajan Singh and Yuvraj Singh. Tamil Nadu government has also announced 3 crore for the winning team and 1 crore for the local boy R Ashwin.

RAILWAY AND AIRBUS AT YOUR SERVICE

Some gave them cash while few handed them land, but there are some who believe in giving the cricketers the best of their services. Railway minister Mamata Banerjee announced that her ministry has decided to give first class AC lifetime passes to all the players. They are allowed unlimited free travel in the railways along with one companion. Banerjee wrote a letter to Dhoni, which said, "It was Swami Vivekananda who said that if one had the will, one could do anything. Even drink an ocean. You and your team have done just that." Rajasthan has announced a complimentary trip on luxurious "Palace On wheels" for all the players. Even, liquor baron Vijay Mallya was not far behind from awarding the world cup heroes of the Indian team. In yet another bonanza for Men in Blue, Kingfisher Airlines announced that the cricketers, their wives and children can avail free lifetime air travel in its carriers both within India and on its international routes.

PROMOTION

To celebrate the glory of world cup win, employers of various cricketers has decided to promote them a notch higher from their previous positions. National carrier Air India has decided to promote four of its employees— skipper Mahendra Singh Dhoni, Yuvraj Singh, Harbhajan Singh and Suresh Raina. Yuvi was moved up from the manager post to the senior manager position while Raina, Dhoni and Bhajji were made managers after getting promotion from the deputy manager post. Public sector Maharatna company Oil and Natural Gas Corporation Ltd. has announced out of turn promotion and a cash prize of Rs. 20 lakh each for the three ONGCian cricketers, Gautam Gambhir, Virat Kohli and Munaf Patel for their stupendous performance in ICC 2011 Cricket World Cup.

BEAUTIES OF ROAD

There are few who are being gifted with beauties on wheels. While Hyundai, the main sponsor of the ICC World Cup, is planning to give each of the players a brand new Hyundai Verna. Audi India has announced that it will present Yuvraj Singh an Audi car in appreciation of his performance in the tournament.

LAND BONANZA

A Rajkot-based builder, Bhupat Bodar, has promised to give a plot of land of 300 square yards to each member of the squad, including coach Gary Kirsten. The Karnataka government has promised to allot free housing sites in Bangalore to each member of the cricket team. Chief minister BS Yeddyurappa was reported as saying, "It's a joyous occasion for the entire country. In recognition of their achievement, the state government will gift free sites measuring 372 square metres (4,000 square feet) in Bangalore soon to all the 15 cricketers." Jharkhand CM Arjun Munda has announced awards for Ranchi boy MS Dhoni, including land given to the captain to set up a cricket academy and school. The Jharkhand government is also planning to confer an honorary doctorate on Dhoni, while the Jharkhand unit of the Congress has even demanded that Dhoni be conferred with the Bharat Ratna. Uttarakhand chief minister Ramesh Pokhriyal Nishank promised a residential plot or a house in Mussoorie for Dhoni and Sachin Tendulkar, who have been a regular visitor there with their family. He also announced that a stadium will be built in the state to be named after skipper Dhoni. Also, Virender Sehwag and Ashish Nehra will be honored with the best sportsperson of the year award of Haryana.

HONORARY COMMISSION IN ARMY

MS Dhoni, the captain of the 'Men in Blue', will now don the olive greens of the Indian Army as he was recently given the honorary rank of an officer as a token of appreciation for his World Cup achievement. Dhoni, along with Suresh Raina, was invited by Army Chief General VK Singh for tea at his residence where he was given the offer, which he accepted.

Jai Ho!

"Jai Ho", "Jai Hind" and "Vande Mataram" was the response of Bollywood celebrities when India beat Sri Lanka to win the cricket World Cup after 28 years. The film fraternity saluted Indian captain MS Dhoni and Sachin Tendulkar, apart from congratulating Sri Lanka for a tough match. The celebrities took to micro-blogging site Twitter to congratulate team India soon after the match ended. Here's some of their tweets:

Chak De India! Until India winning the World Cup the tattoo 'D' on my hand was meant for "Don 2" but from now it would mean skipper M.S. Dhoni.

— *Shah Rukh Khan*

Congrats Team India!!! We did it!!!! Great job bringing the cup back!!! Strong work Dhoni, Tendulkar and company! What an awesome match. Both sides played well!

— *Madhuri Dixit*

Yayyyyyyy!!!! What a historic moment! I'm so lucky to be here and see this happen live in front of my eyes! I've never experienced this kind of mass hysteria!!! India is proud of our team: jai hind!

— *Vivek Oberoi*

And History is made! A timeless moment which will be etched in our minds forever. Well done team India, take a bow. U made us cry n made r dream come true

— *Shilpa Shetty*

Celebrities tweets on India's World Cup victory

Wow what a win! Congratulation Indian team you are supreme. Dhoni, what a fight back. Aap sab jeete raho. U makes us burst with pride.
— *Shabana Azmi*

Mahi and our entire team made us so proud! What a historical moment! The excitement was unimaginable!
— *Bipasha Basu*

Chak De India!!! Congratulations to the team and thankyou!!! That's 28yrs in the coming! Unbelievable stuff!!
— *Lara Dutta*

"Thank you team India for giving us this glorious and proud moment. Jai Ho"
— *Anupam Kher*

"Thank you Sri lanka for making it tough! YOU played so well! Made our win so much sweeter!"
— *Diya Mirza*

India creates history, winning the World Cup. Such proud moments for every Indian. Congrats Team India. Jai Hind & Vande Mataram. In Mohali it was Dussehra and in Mumbai it is Diwali.
— *Madhur Bhandarkar*

"Sachin will finally be able to hold that one piece of Silverware that has evaded him his whole career...A WC trophy!!! AWESOME win! So proud of our team. So proud to be Indian!"
— *Mandira Bedi*

"Incredible! It's like we just won our independence. It is madness outside!! Abhishek, Aishwarya and me on top of the roof of car, waving tricolor and just screaming."
— *Amitabh Bachchan*

"Congrats India!!! Awesome win :) We are the champions Jai ho!!!"
— *Arbaaz Khan*

Proudest

Indian cricketers have made their families proud with their world cup win. These loved ones are the pillars, who have given away everything to make the dream of their lads a reality. Here is what the family's said after this famous win.

I was left speechless. I couldn't believe that India had finally won. Yuhoooo and we have done it was Yuvi's first reaction over phone when he rang me up. It's an incredible feeling, yet to sink in. I am feeling like I am over the moon, simply overwhelmed.

— *Shabnam Singh, Yuvraj Singh's Mother*

I am very happy. In fact I don't have words to describe how I am feeling. I can't believe what has happened. We will celebrate once he comes back.

— *Saroj Kohli, Virat Kohli's Mother*

I am very excited. I switched off the TV after he (Sehwag) got out. Switched it on only in the last 15 overs. But I had the intuition that we would win the World Cup.

— *Aarti Sehwag, Virender Sehwag's Wife*

Families

I am so happy for India and proud of my son. His father was a fan of this game. He wanted Bhajji to take up this sport. I don't know too much about this game. Now I have checked out some girls for him. His two sisters have been married off, now it is his turn to get married.

— *Avtar Kaur, Harbhajan Singh's Mother*

I think I will hug him and probably weep over his shoulders. He has made all of us so proud. God bless you my son, you have made the nation and a father proud. It was my dream of 30 years to live for this moment. If ever there is a second birth, I will like you to be born as my son again so that I could give you all the happiness and comfort which I deprived you during your child-hood to see you become a top cricketer.

— *Yograj Singh, Yuvraj Singh's Father*

"Gautam is a great player. I have no regrets about him missing the century. Today he was playing for the team. Everybody has to contribute. This is amazing."

— *Seema Gambhir, Gautam Gambhir's Mother*

"Congrats to Mahi and Sakshi. I spoke to them last night and congratulated them. They are celebrating, so we don't want to disturb them."

— *Sheila Singh, MS Dhoni's Mother-in-Law*

RECORDS MILES

SECOND TIME

India ended their 28-year title drought in World Cup by beating Sri Lanka by six wickets in the final at Wankhede Stadium, Mumbai. It was India's second title victory in World Cup. Their first title win came under Kapil Dev when they beat West Indies in the final at Lord's on June 25, 1983.

FIRST WICKET-KEEPER

Mahendra Singh Dhoni became the first wicket-keeper ever to lead his team to title victory in a World Cup.

$ 3.3 MILLION PRIZE MONEY

Indian cricket team became richer by more than $3.3 million (about Rs 16 crore) by winning the World Cup. Mahi's team got a cheque of $ 3250000 (about Rs 15 crore) for winning the final match. The remaining amount of $ 135,000 came from their four wins and a tie in the league stages.

100 TIMES MORE

When it comes to prize money, out of the total of Rs 46 lakh (calculated according to current exchange rate), Kapil Dev's team pocketed Rs 14 lakh in 1983. Mahendra Singh Dhoni's team got a cheque 100 times larger, of about Rs 16 crore. The tournament's total prize money was Rs 40 crore ($ 8.1 million).

& TONES

HIGHEST IN THE FINAL

Gautam Gambhir's 97 was the highest score by an Indian batsman in World Cup final. Virender Sehwag who made 82 against Australia at Johannesburg on March 23, 2003 held the previous record.

FIRST BATSMAN TO SCORE 18000

Sachin Tendulkar became the first batsman ever to score 18000 runs in limited overs international cricket. The Master blaster reached this milestone during his 53-run knock in the second quarter final of the 10th World Cup against Australia at Sardar Patel Stadium, Motera, Ahmedabad on March 24. It was the 440th inning of his 451st match in one day internationals. Sachin Tendulkar who made his one day international debut against Pakistan at Gujranwala on December 18,1989, took 21 years and 96 days to reach to this landmark.

FIFTH INDIAN TO SCORE 8000

Yuvraj Singh became the fifth Indian and 23rd batsman overall to score 8000 runs in ODIs. The left hand middle order batsman achieved this feat after completing his 30th run during his unbeaten 57-run knock against Australia in the quarter final. It was the 250th inning of his 272nd match in ODIs.

THIRD INDIAN SKIPPER TO COMPLETE CENTURY

MS Dhoni became the third Indian skipper after Mohammed Azharuddin (174 matches) and Sourav Ganguly (147 matches) and 15th player overall to lead a team in 100 or more matches in one day international cricket. The quarter final match against Australia was Mahi's 100th as captain in one dayers.

103

FIRST TO SCORE SIX TONS IN WORLD CUP

Sachin Tendulkar became the first batsman to score six centuries in World Cup. The master blaster achieved this feat by making 111 off 101 balls with eight fours and three sixes against South Africa at Vidarbha Cricket Association Stadium, Jamtha, Nagpur on March 12. The master blaster also became the first batsman to score 2000 runs in World Cup.

FIRST ALL ROUNDER EVER

Yuvraj Singh became the third Indian after K.Srikkanth and Sourav Ganguly and 14th all-rounder overall to score a fifty and take five wickets in a one day international match by taking five wickets for 31 runs and scoring an unbeaten 50 against Ireland at M Chinnaswamy Stadium, Bangalore on March 6. He is the first player ever to do the same in a World Cup match.

ZAHEER KHAN'S FEAT

Zaheer Khan set an Indian record of most wickets in a single World Cup by taking 21 wickets at 18.76 in 9 matches. Roger Binny who claimed 18 wickets at 18.66 in eight matches in 1983 held the previous record. Zaheer Khan also equalled Javagal Srinath's Indian record of most wickets in World Cups by taking his 44th wicket in the final. Javagal Srinath also claimed the same number of wickets in 34 matches. Zaheer Khan has played in only 23 World Cup matches.

FIRST INDIAN

Virat Kohli became the first Indian and 13th batsman overall to score a hundred while playing in his first match in the World Cup. He made an unbeaten 100 off 83 balls against Bangladesh at Dhaka which was India's third fastest century and joint eighth in World Cup cricket.

MOST SIXES

Sachin Tendulkar set an Indian record of hitting most sixes in World Cups by hitting his first six during his 111-run knock against South Africa at Nagpur on March 12. Sachin Tendulkar's 27 sixes in 44 innings of 45 matches is the joint third highest in World Cups. Sourav Ganguly, who had hit 25 sixes in 21 innings of as many matches, held the previous Indian record.

EDEN GARDENS, INDIA'S BIGGEST STADIUM, HAS A CAPACITY OF 1 LAC. OUR CAPACITY IS 29.15 LAC.